THE PLUMB LINE

Hélène Demetriades

First published 2022 by The Hedgehog Poetry Press

Published in the UK by
The Hedgehog Poetry Press
5, Coppack House
Churchill Avenue
Clevedon
BS21 6QW

www.hedgehogpress.co.uk

ISBN: 978-1-913499-33-4

Contents

BEGINNINGS

For Fiona Benson

THUMB TALK

She didn't suck me
when she was born
but later, strip by strip
she skinned me
with her teeth.

I was a miniature megalith
on red alert
sheathed in a black leather
thumbstall
tied to her wrist.

GHOST MOTHER

I'm on the abacus – red
orange yellow blue green
doing my times-tables –
I falter at the line of hurdles –
Daddy hits me says I'm stupid.

I run down the garden;
my brother is flying on a swing.
I brush my legs against the fluff-white
of dead flowers, scrape a stick
across the rusty swing-frame.

At bedtime I crumple
under the thick hotel eiderdown.
Too late my mother touches
my shoulder with her hand.

A DISGRACE

I throw-up on my Sunday dress
winding down
        from the Rocher du Midi
to the city by the lake
            Daddy erupts
Mummy bundles me out of the train
            we're going to Yaya's for lunch
    We buy another frock
            white-knitted with pom poms
I lift the heavy tea-pot   miss the china cup
    spill Darjeeling all over the tablecloth
            burn the back of my hand
Daddy boils over   *She's so clumsy!*
    I watch my skin curl away
like wave froth on sand

IN MY WORLD

Let me slip past an old orchard,
past chalets which creak in the breeze
skip down the hill to school

in a bright blue cardigan,
April unbuttoned, the quilt
of snow thrown off.

There's a rat corpse on the wall,
I catch my breath at the heave-sea
flesh, maggots devouring it to bone tracery.

I bob up beyond the cable car track,
past the dachshund at the doctor's
meshed gate, his bright square of lawn;

cross the high street, skim past the kiosk,
the red and gold foil-wrapped têtes-choco,
to school.

At lunch, on the way home, I'll buy one,
bite into the dark chocolate cranium
tongue plunging into sticky froth,

and at the dipped crossroads, my best friend and I,
we'll sip from the fountain's spout, sit on the lip
of the stone trough, dangling our legs in eternity

eyeing the dark chalet abutting
the gush-rock stream – hearts skipping a beat –
because that's where the witch lives.

CHEZ MADAME FRISE

I ride on her swing
        my feet touching mountains
play with her lodgers
        search for stripy snails in her log pile

There's a basket of kittens
        by the boiler
slices of *pain et chocolat*
        on the table

If you carry on I'll give you an injection
        she says if we're naughty

She drowns the kittens
        in a trough full of tadpoles

At eight
    I have a puff of cigarette
        in the toilet upstairs

My friend Simonetta
        shows me her crop
of black pubic hair

    In the attic a teenage lodger
pins me to the floor
    wrestles with my zip

When I leave   Madame Frise gives me
a loved cat
    with a worn nose
        and missing eye

THE PLAYGROUND

The year we left the mountains

a new playground was set
            among young trees

            on the other side
of the road from the gushing stream

a red slide shiny roundabout set of swings

We scaled the birches for a dare
    curious
            where our pee would fall

        Mine spilt
            down the silver trunk
                    like a christening

I didn't recognise it
            as my future grief

            a torrent of burning water
for the land I would lose

EAST PRESTON

Not able to recite my alphabet or pronounce *th*,
writing *futparf* in my school book
I shrink in the low-ceilinged prefab.
Are you Cockney? a child asks in swimming class.
I lack the inner or outer geography to know.

On a pebble beach draining into grey sea
a place so desolate I feel my life has died
I long for the mountains,
the green belly of my village.

I miss my best friend, Anne,
the bright colours of Swiss autumn,
the soft cheese, *Petit Suisse*
sugar-sweet-delicious.
Digestive biscuits are strange and sandy.

WHITEGATES (I)

A gravel half-moon, wisteria across the porch,
a pear tree too tired to fruit, and in a fork
the robin's nest quilted with border collie hair.

There's a baby bath dug into the ground
where tadpoles' tails are eaten by water boatmen,
the raspberry cage where Daddy stones a blackbird.

We have Persian rugs on parquet floors,
a gilt chariot clock driven by cherubs.
Playboy magazines are tucked into the bureau.

The playroom houses the dog and black & white TV,
the kitchen a chequered floor
where I cower, small pawn, arm across my face.

PYJAMA CASE

At night Bucephalus *
tucks his long legs by my side
the white star on his forehead shining
through darkness – the secret hours
where I breathe uncensored.

Come morning I stuff his flat belly
with my soft entrails.
Zip him up for the day.

* *Alexander the Great's famous stallion.*

17

BLUE SKY

If only that woolly cloud
were tied to her wrist
like a balloon at the end of a party.

She would walk home tall,
offer it to her mother.

Anchored in the kitchen
it would buoy *Mummy.*

The girl imagines snuggling into it,
the softness
spilling out of her hands.

THE ALUMINIUM GRATER

Mum clamps the grater onto the worktop,
drives the cheese chunks into its mouth,
turns the handle rotating the drum.

The sharp holes worm the cheese
into the white bowl.

Mum is the star I revolve around.
She leans into the grater daily
bolstering herself,
I spin away.

ON BEING SENT AWAY TO SCHOOL

I'll be glad to get rid of you!

Later I'm standing at my bedroom window,
below my father is weeding the rockery.

This time Mum has intervened.
He has something to say to you.

He looks up,
I'm sorry for what I said. It was wrong of me.

Our eyes meet.
I pull back from the window
rudderless
our relationship peeled bare.

THE ARRIVAL

Ahead of me the trunk sways
like a coffin down the corridors.

My parents heave it up the stairs,
drop it onto the dormitory floor.

A crater opens between us.

Retracing our steps, I see them off
at the school entrance –

turn back to unpack my loss.

Stuff it into drawers under my allotted bed,
hang it limp in the dark of communal wardrobes.

That night I lie in a row of girls
with no walls on either side
to stop me from falling

WEEKENDS

On Saturdays we herd like calves
round the dark table, thirsting for post.

On Sundays we are walked two by two
up Chinthurst Hill, inmates in uniform.

The sounds of TV matinees spill
against common room walls,
air void of family
presses against rib-cages.

In chapel we score senior girls' outfits,
let loose we trail through a gut
of empty corridors.

The toilet cubicles smell of bleach,
the medicated loo paper is thin and shiny.
On it I discover the smear of my first bleed.

LETTER FROM HOME

You wrote that you felt lonely
on the drive home without me.
Whitegates was very quiet.

Kiwi was being cared for,
I needn't worry –
you were picking her milk-thistles.
Papillon had lost her balance,
was swimming upside down.

Andrew had written you a cheerful letter,
was settling in nicely,
Anna had phoned home –
you were sad to hear I wasn't happy.

You wrote I should make a real effort
 – you knew how hard it was –
you'd been to boarding-school,
hadn't seen your parents in months.

I shouldn't be glum, it wasn't so distressing
– in front of my classmates and teachers
I'd want to put my brave face on.

Besides you'd always be here to advise
– once I was willing to accept my new life
I'd get a taste for it –

and not having Daddy around
would be a relief.

PLAYING DEAD

Girls tickle my legs, waist, under my arms,
squeeze toothpaste into my nostrils,
try to prize open my teeth.

Rigor mortis makes me triumphant
in the game on the dormitory floor.

At home I fell out of bed
too afraid to cry out to my mother
who slept next to an ogre.

I lay on the floor
squeezing my anus
tight as a rosebud.

WEEKLY HAIR WASH

They laughed at Goldballs in his blue overalls
pressing his body into their backs as they sat
in a chair craning their necks over the basin,
warm water trickling over their napes,
the caress of his hands on their heads,
this sixty-something-year-old man with pale eyes
fingering pre-teen scalps, wiping his snot in their hair.

ORCHID CACTUS

I bought a stub of wretched cactus
from the church jumble sale.
It grew into a giant spider on my window sill.
Scarlet flowers flared from serrated stems,
luminous lime centres dripped nectar
anthers and filaments panting like tongues.

Home from boarding school
I found it shrivelled in the greenhouse.
My father had taken against its unruly ways.

CAGED

An ogre has fashioned a cheese dome
out of his thoughts – brought it
down on a family.

Inside there's fancy furniture,
an airing cupboard and parquet floors.

The little people are clay in his smooth hands.
The mother cooks *osso bucco,* dreams
of tap dancing on the Pavilion stage.

There's a teenage girl sitting on her bed
munching through packets of Jaffa Cakes.

She'll shed the layers like baggy jumpers
back at boarding school.

STOLEN TIME

You were the cousin who took me out of school
for long weekends. We saw the band Secret Affair
and a 1950s black and white French film.

We shared the same bed in your Charlton digs,
slurped each other in,
drove round to your friends for dope.

You spoke to me about your clingy girlfriend,
your failed drumming career.

We sunbathed on the Isle of Wight,
saw the Picasso in London,
went to the pub in Plumpton.

Your postcards were the Pied Piper's calling cards:
Van Gogh poppies, Samuel Palmer moons,
a Constable windmill.

You said you'd take me to New York.

MY SISTER TAKES A HAPPY FAMILY PHOTO

Behind us wisteria rampages
over the white façade.

My arm's round Mum's waist,
she's bending into me like a reed,
curly head tilted, beaming at my brother

who's standing apart
hand in his pocket
looking straight at the camera.

My father's hooked in on my other side
turning his neck to leer at his son
– I think it's the beard.

My eyes are half-closed
in a plump face,
bright bag and shaggy coat
spilling over my arm

head jerked back
like a horse refusing to jump.

APPEASEMENT

My brother rattles the match box, threatens
to burn down the chalet if I don't play Mousetrap.
I go along with him, buy time
till Mum comes home from the shops.

I'm invited to a viewing spot near Florence,
Lorenzo's hand swoops to my knee –
trapped in the front seat
I become his confidante, ask about his gran.

In Brittany a man draws out his penis,
begs me to rub his chest while he wanks.
No I'm not doing that, I say to the windscreen.
He moans, climaxes, wipes himself on a Kleenex
bursts into tears; drives me back to town
for tea and cakes.

MY FUNNY VALENTINE

Although you chase me
up the stairs laughing
and tickle me as I hide
behind my door frightened,
your hand up my nightdress,
and you send me a Valentine
of a man baby holding a heart
over his genitals, and he's blushing
and the card is saying,
*IF YOU CAN'T BE GOOD
BE MINE,*
and although you visit me years later,
and we're admiring the roses
in Greenwich Park and the bees
on the flowers, and you're saying,
Be careful, they're going to pollinate you,
and in the back of the cab you tease me,
The driver will think I'm your beau,
(although excuse me, you're 80*),*
you are my father.

GRAVITY

for Gavin & Kaia

GRACE

Trailing the paths of a London park
    like a half-lit ghost
        grieving a foetus
I crawl under the skirts of a rhododendron

        and enter a womb
  of thrumming blooms
      where branches are snakes
          and sunlight is filtering through pink

      A bee homes in on my dress
as if I too am a blossom
    The O of my ovum shudders dilates
It will swallow the earth

REWILDING

The holly tree squats in mud
    blood fresh
against bright Dartmoor blue

When I was born
    I slipped my footing
        fell eyes first into the lonely heart
of my flame-haired mother

The holly's seeds ripen on her crown
    mine are buried deep
but I flower just like her

28 HOURS

The world sleeps
and foxes are screaming in the garden.

On the bedroom floor
my body cramps.

In the early hours the midwife
reaches inside me, touches my baby's hair.

*If you don't buck up
this won't go well for you.*

My baby's spine presses into mine,
my rump's about to split.

I shuffle up and down the stairs
to shift baby and pelvis.

Her heart decelerates.
Rush hour, time to leave home.

Clutching the back seat of the car
I stare out at the world turning without me.

KEEPING YOU CLOSE

Here you are: eyes clenched,
face smeared in white greasepaint.

The subtlest tremor behind your eyes
when I touch the top of your head.

Now gone.

I'm wheeled into a side room,
stitched up, left waiting.

The anaesthetist arrives, asks,
Where's the baby?

Later I see photos of your first hour:
waxy fists, red lips, gummy eyes now ajar,
bawling at your father; the midwife mired
in official forms, wrapping up his shift.

That night on the ward dark figures loom
in spectral succession at the end of my bed
admonishing me for keeping you
tucked to my chest.

PLACENTA

Laid out on the floorboards
an autumn tree crown
rises skyward
from a severed trunk.

A glistening viscus
grown by mother and daughter
brought home in a carrier bag
preserved in the freezer.
Planted out in spring
– now pulsing through the earth.

THE FIRST DAYS

I'm born into service. My womb darns herself,
nipples crack open, weep.

I look at you asleep, lying open to the world
arms flung above your head in the middle of our bed
twitching as your body fires up, settles in.

My mouth gapes. I'm like a fish in the bedroom
gasping for words

THOSE 4PM BLUES

That void between tea-time and dinner
stranded on the settee
with nothing to hold on to
but my baby daughter

That gulf at the end of the school day
with no home to go back to

I forego the sticky willy iced buns,
the chatter of tea,
repair to the dormitory, transition to mufti.
Taste that empty pocket of space

before trooping to classroom for prep,
chapel to pray

GROWING PAINS

We breastfed our babies, grew our friendship
in my lean-to conservatory. We were pioneers
taking buggies and picnics up the long hill to the park
our children staining purple under the mulberry trees.

At Botany Bay my toddler took tentative steps
across sand tugged by your daughter.

Later I got ill, I heard you were worried.
You didn't visit, we chose different schools;
I left voice messages.

One day I bumped into you outside
our favourite cafe.
I was angry. Perhaps I looked scary.

I don't need you anymore, I've got Becca now, you said.

It was as if I'd been run over by a train.

QUESTION TIME

Will I still be me with my skin off?
Naked she's tugging
an invisible hem at her waist.

At night a wolf attacks her in her sleep.
Mummy! Mummy! she cries out
to the figure receding down the corridor.

Swallowed in the gulp of an instant
she hears herself
hum like an electric cable.

*Why do I feel safe
looking up at the stars?*
she says years later watching Mars.

REMEMBRANCE DAY

We dip our hands in sweet almond oil and herbs,
work our love and shame
into the candles we rub between our palms,
calling out the names of our aborted
and miscarried children, Anemone, Ajax.

We light our candles, push them in their birchwood holders,
surround them with gentians, and bluebells from the garden.
We give our babies chocolate ladybirds and elephants.

We place them in the sun, by the sliding doors
to keep an eye on them, as we tip-toe in the kitchen
in awe of our new charges, burning down.

BECOMING INVISIBLE

A moth caterpillar crawls in russet and black
across a cold flagstone. I crouch, my finger
touching the tips of its hairs, but when I kneel
closer it tucks in its face, stills, miniature bottle brush,
as if without movement or face it could cancel itself –
like my daughter age five throwing a handful
of earth into her father's supper, delighted –
then daunted by his rare anger, sliding behind
the bamboo to hide her flushed face, legs poking out.

MY DAUGHTER BOUNCES AHEAD LIKE A BALL

How small my breasts have become,
two little dumplings, no signs of shrinkage,
the stretch marks have all but disappeared.

I am not ready to leave this sun-dried earth,
I thought my narrow tray of gifts would be enough.
I must line my hems with weights.

RAPUNZEL

She never clung
to a favourite teddy bear,
never sucked her thumb.

Now aged fourteen
she carries her hairbrush everywhere
brushing her newly resplendent locks
in preparation for departure.

MOTHER & DAUGHTER

There's flowers in here,
my daughter babbled
suckling at the breast.

Lions, we roared on all fours
across her bedroom floor.

Now I trip over worn clothes,
sticky noodle pots;
am ordered out
tail between my legs.

GOODIES

My daughter is radiant at noon.
Sunday morning shop girl
home with an armful of groceries
from the village store.

Use-by-today doughnuts,
chocolate croissants, Co-op pizza,
tenderstem broccoli for me.

My father came home from the City
with fresh walnuts in his briefcase,
bags of dusky pistachios from Greece,
Gruyère cheese from La Suisse.

Every evening the kitchen was filled
with his bounty and tyranny.

THE YOUNG WOMAN

She's a tiger pacing its cell
finger pads smearing windows
and walls.

She's the heavy footed Yeti
crashing up and down stairs.

At times she chuckles to herself
– the world beyond
beating through her airpods.

BIRTH PANGS

My daughter is eighteen today.
From the cliff top dolphins
are breaching the sea in pairs,
here, there and everywhere!
A few toss themselves up
like party poppers.

My waters broke four days early.
I was speaking to my mother on the phone.

The midwives monitored my baby's
private pool, swabbed its leaking
waters for infection.

 Now my daughter is a child again
jumping rocks above a bubbling sea.
She turns and calls –

DEPARTURE

for my mother & father

IN SOLITUDE TOGETHER

You at the river's edge, your walking stick
and painful hip, me wading to the spot
where the rivers' join, turning my head,
catching your eye. This is our church –
the quietness of the river's gush and pour,
the sullen rocks, a mother's longing
for her daughter beyond the hailstone chatter.

UNDER FIRE

Pammy rescues worms
   rebeds them in-side-of-road soil
picks up discarded flowers
   lays them to sleep in the Thames.
Her mummy took her to France on holiday
   and swapped her for a lover.

     On deck she holds hands with her little sister
   looks through the railings towards Dover
      the wind rises   the sea spumes
   they wobble like jetsam
      a nanny buttons up their jackets.

I'm leaning in to wash her hair;
     hunched over the kitchen sink
she's a baby bird.
       Her skull is a steel helmet.

THE LAST SUPPER

She punctures the boiled tomato,
taps the plate,
lifts a forkful of rice to her mouth.

Slips on the rubber gloves,
turns on the tap, scrubs and stacks
the pans to the whistling kettle.

Unscrews the decaf,
bites into a square of dark chocolate.

Enters the day in her diary
scraping tip across paper.

Pushes the walking frame ahead,
sits down on her mother's sofa,
presses the remote.

The sound of the news,
the sound of her retching,
the soft thud sideways onto cushions.

Next day, the caretaker's key in the lock.

YELLOW PERIWINKLES ON HER COFFIN

I'm hammering in the tent pegs,
don't pick up my brother's messages.

Later he tells me how they attached her to a monitor,
how the doctor said, *No signs of life in her brain,*
yet her left hand crossed over to her right arm,
raised and dropped its dead weight;
plucked at the bed clothes, lifted her nightdress.

I'm collecting periwinkles on the beach.
He pops out to buy a toothbrush.

She untethers.

FALLING TO EARTH

i
My mother dead. I stagger into a sunset
over the Scilly Isles
and soaked in life beyond biology
I discover she is me.

ii
Mid-summer yet cherry blossoms wake,
blackbirds sing in white orchards.
The air and earth are soft with falling blooms
as if I'd just been born.
Her scentless scent is everywhere.

iii
I expected dust but she is granular.
I burrow into the weighty sand,
cradle her in my palm.
I lift her with a silver-plated tablespoon,
transfer her to a heart-shaped urn,
find alloy pins amongst the ash.

WHITEGATES (II)

The privet hedge has been uprooted,
vistas opened. I step out of the car,
look through the tall pine trunks
to the curved lawn now studded with box balls
along its flint wall, the front door painted
a Farrow & Ball Cooking Apple Green
cerise hydrangeas against the white front.
The courtyard where my rabbit lived is a carport.

In that house a presence bit into the base of my skull
crippling me as I lay in bed. And I called out to Gavin,
Switch the light on!
But the bulb had blown so we went downstairs,
fiddled with the fuse box and floodlit the lounge.
I swiped the tarry entity off my back,
threw it into my other hand where it clung
searing a blister – and was gone.

A VISIT FROM MY MOTHER

The doll-eyed 9-year-old sits on a Paris pony
bare-thighed, jacket ribboned at her throat.

Tonight she comes to me as an elder
striding across the plains of death,
the horse Abdullah at her side like one
of the big cats, legs shorter than in life
ears pricked forward, nose nudging me.

In the day-bright dream
I cradle his enraptured face,
wish to keep him for the winter,
ride him in Greenwich Park.

You'll need to know how to saddle him.
I know, I say, *pull the girth in twice.*

HAWK

My father has hooded eyes and a hooked nose.
He cocks his head to contemplate his quarry.

A solitary man – he seeks freedom in the mountains,
soars on his skis.

Fascinated by the bright plumage in park aviaries
he eyes the Ara macaws in their cage.

He too has clipped wings – his soul is outraged.

LOOKING FOR MY FATHER NEAR TAKSIM SQUARE

I'm craning my head, looking for a boy
leaping across the roofs
in mid-air fights with older boys,
kite tails tangling
plunging to the ground –

I sidle into a bric a brac shop
searching for an anchor,

find an antique album,
Souvenir de Constantinople. *

The broken spine opens onto
tinted images of Galata Bridge,
seas, caiques, towers and mosques

– his first memory
a young woman's severed head
at the foot of a snowy dustbin –

It's for my father's 100th,
he was born on this street.
A Greek...

The vendor tells me it's very expensive.

In a village above a Swiss lake
my father leafs through the images
of the home he's never returned to.

It's rather grubby.
Wraps it back in the tissue paper.

---

* *Constantinople was officially renamed Istanbul in 1930, after the fall of the Ottoman Empire. From 1915 onwards the ethnic minorities of Asia Minor were expelled from their homeland. Some through death marches, others through an exchange of populations.*

FIRST STEPS

They slide you out of bed, your legs
as useless as a puppet's now.

I'm not going! you say as the taxi rolls
you to a nursing home.

Set down in a bare room,
caught between two wheels
without your fine antiques,
you, the man I've been so afraid of.

You must feel very lonely.
Yes! Very!

A surge of life bolts through me as I look at you
– tomorrow I'm flying home.

From the balcony the vineyards rise steeply
up the hill, a viaduct vaults terraces,
I long to reach it, surprise you.

I kiss you and climb – my legs yours now.

Near the top I phone you, *Dad! Dad!*
Come out on the balcony! Look up the hill!
Can you see me waving?

I'm taking my first steps.

You mutter, hesitate, then, *Oh yes!*
Laughter in my ear.

Striding through the goldened terraces
I wave goodbye above the lake.

On the phone next day in different countries
you confess you hadn't really seen me.

ERRANDS FOR AN ELDERLY FATHER

Criss-crossing Lausanne
free pass in my pocket
I fly on errands from point to point.
Gliding on trolley buses
unburdened,
I'm held in a network of numbers and timings
joining at junctions.

With each interlude the sun is up
on curved wooden benches
at the bus stop.

WHEELCHAIR ACCESS

I longed to share the places
that drew you in your daily life
mapping out your spirograph of town,
intimate mandala of your *va-et-vient*.

Lausanne's newsagents, restaurants,
sleek shops and banks, that catered
for your necessities and the delicacies:
the *Herald Tribune*, smoked salmon,
Bally shoes, Lombard Odier.

I am grateful for these years,
your wheelchair has allowed me access.
We've sat on café terraces
soaking up the sun,
shopped for trousers
and a pair of dark green slip-ons.
Navigated pavement edges
breached old divides.

THE PLUMB LINE

Father, I lift your thinning thighs, nudge
down your trousers, peel off your socks,
slide over satin skin, tenderised
by your ancient flesh.

Tonight in our goodbyes you stutter,
B-b-bless you for protecting me.

In the early hours I wake,
words flooding my mouth:
It's not me, it's not me
the safe-keeper,
it's the plumb line between us.

FINAL CALL

Remove my specs I can't kiss you otherwise.

I feel a tenderness land on my cheek
beyond his gnarledness
and beyond my guard against the years of hurts
I receive his kiss and feel the us of everything.

As I leave the marbled foyer
                                        through sliding glass
            opening and closing
                        opening and closing
                                    between us

he raises his arms and calls down the path,
                        Lots of love for ever and ever,
lots of love for ever and ever.

IN THE WINGS

Enter stage left
A new resident wheels
himself into my father's room
huffing like a lost bear
taking centre stage.

Stage right
Bent over his remote
Dad seems not to notice
but at dinner surprises me:
That man's been paying me visits.

Offstage
Stagehands hover in the unlit
fringes of my father's existence.
He glances to the right.
They're not ready for me yet.

PARTING GIFT

In this season of extended siestas
my father marinades
in the womb of his wheelchair,
punctures the silence of his room,
Aie.......... aie...............aie

His eyes have diluted,
but when I pop strawberries in his mouth
he smacks his lips
and pummels out the juices with his gums.

Sliding my fingers over his hand
– I catch my breath –
his eyes are flaring like dying suns.

Unable to endure that deepening glow
I say, *That's a lovely smile!*

He shrinks, his upper lip curls.
I can't smile, I don't have any teeth.

DADDYKINS

When they turn you over
to remove your sodden nappy
you moan and coil
into a foetal skeleton.

I stroke your cheeks,
whisper you sweet nothings,
sing you broken bits of nursery rhyme.

Conjure you into a loving daddy
with my breath.

FAMILIAL INTIMACY

We are chugging to your death
on the panting rhythm of your breath.

I crush lavender buds under your nose –
you open your mouth like a baby bird.

You sleep with eyes wide, gaze turned in.
I see into depths without being checked.

On day three your eyes break the surface.
Your lips are moving. I lean in.

You're hopeless! you hiss.
You are the death adder, *Acanthophis.*

I flee your bedside. You slip back
into your body's fevered decoupling.

YOUR LAST HOURS

Outside, lightning bleaches the sky purple.
Inside, my ears grope for your breath.

I lean in, tip the sippy cup to your lips.
Your face is glowing like foxfire.

The following day, a second wind
I spoon you a mocha ice-cream

but sticky secretions bubble up
in your throat
like a subterranean spring
swallowing you.

Help me! Help me! you cry out.

At last a nurse is here tucking
morphine into your vein,
smoothing you to a glazed torpor.

At teatime I'm singing to you:
Gate, gate, paragate,
parasamgate, bodhi svaha! *

Your ears and eyes widen, tilting
like sunflowers towards day.

You suck in air pumping your chest
on the frontline of death.

You breathe in and out, in and out,
eyes flooding the room with white light.

I look into you
and blown to the widest wonder
you leave on an inbreath.

* *Gone, gone, gone beyond, gone utterly beyond, what an awakening! Amen!*

AN ALEMBIC ON THE THRESHOLD

I sing as your body shuts down,
watch the doors of your mind
fly off their hinges
a white sun pulsing through your eyes,
your chest an alembic
gathering you with each breath you suck in,
I witness your birth as you die
as you suck in your last breath elated,
finally fully alive
and you don't expire, but keep hold
of your breath and take wing
as I gaze into your brilliant face on the bed
not knowing you've left, mesmerised.

POSTHUMOUS

My father's face sets

           in   slow   motion

     his   skin   tightens

turns   to   stone

his eyes are polyhedrons

       they *glitter*

I'm gazing at the mask of a Greek monster

ACKNOWLEDGEMENTS

To the editors of the following magazines, webzines & anthologies in which some of these poems first appeared, with grateful thanks.
Acid Bath Press, Allegro, Dreich, Dream Catcher, Envoi, Ink Sweat & Tears, Lemon Peel Press, Marsden the Poetry Village competition anthology, Obsessed With Pipework, One Hand Clapping, Poetry Shed, Poetry Village, Reach Poetry, Snakeskin, The Lake.

Madame Frise & A Visit From my Mother were commended in the Poetry Teignmouth Competition 2021.

Wheelchair Access was highly commended in Marsden the Poetry Village Competition 2019.

An Alembic on the Threshold was shortlisted in the Wells Festival of Literature Open Poetry Competition 2021.

The Last Hours was highly commended in the International Poetry on The Lake competition 2021.

With thanks and gratitude to:

Fiona Benson, for her enormous generosity, encouragement and close reading of the poems.

Katrina Naomi for her editing eye.

Veronica Aaronson, editing buddy, for walking the journey with me.

Fiona, Katrina, Eve Grubin and Martin Figura for their kind comments, and for taking the time to read my manuscript.

Poetry tutors, including: Fiona Benson, Katrina Naomi, Julie-ann Rowell, Greta Stoddart, Eve Grubin, Rebecca Gethin, Wayne Holloway-Smith, Rebecca Varley-Winter, Hannah Lowe, and to fellow poetry class participants for their suggestions and feedback.

Rupert Spira, who urged me to keep writing.

Abbi Torrance for the front cover design & photo.

Mark Davidson at Hedgehog for choosing to publish my collection.

And with gratitude to my husband, Gavin, for his love, encouragement and input, and to my daughter, Kaia, for being, irrepressibly, herself.

PRAISE FOR HÉLÈNE DEMETRIADES

"Hélène Demetriades' *The Plumb Line* is a magnificent, soaring testament to the tenacity of the human spirit. These are powerful, visionary poems, attentive to the body and the dark and tender places of the soul. They probe our closest human relationships, and are both raw to harm, and deeply compassionate. By the end of *The Plumb Line* I found myself inspired and consoled by the human capacity for love, which is something beyond forgiveness, and by the power of poetry to interrogate, transcend and transform."

- *Fiona Benson.*

"In these poems, the things of this world—'Persian rugs on parquet floors', 'a trough full of tadpoles', 'a gush-rock stream'—are imbued with an other-worldly richness. At the same time, the poems struggle and are grounded in the ordeals of childhood and growing up. The reader dips into this rich world with awe and wonder, 'dangling our legs', with the speaker of these poems, 'in eternity'."

- *Eve Grubin*

"Hélène Demetriades' courageous, gendered poems in *The Plumb Line* question how women are seen and not seen. Love and compassion float above a powerful undertow of violence and unease."

- *Katrina Naomi*

"This is no fairy tale, the ogre is an only too real father, the pages 'filled with his bounty and tyranny'. The fragility of childhood is laid bare in powerful poems that spare nothing in their startling physicality. A daughter performs a kind of alchemy and remarkably a love 'scented with lavender buds' survives the stoniest of grounds."

- *Martin Figura*